Cute & Adorable Cat Colouring Books

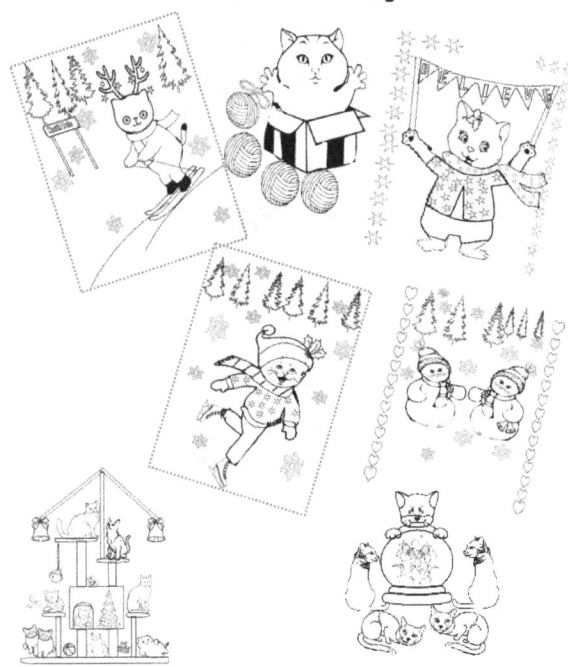

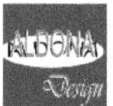

We Would appreciate your Opinion
About this book by leaving a
Review
link follows
www.amazon.com/author/aldonadesign

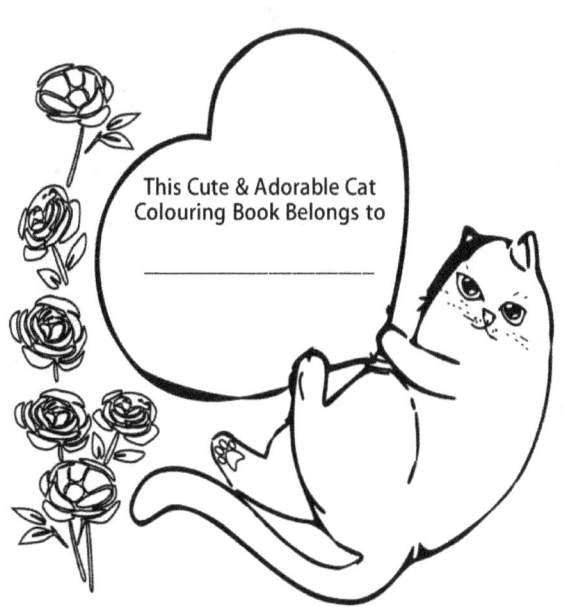

This Cute & Adorable Cat
Colouring Book Belongs to

_____

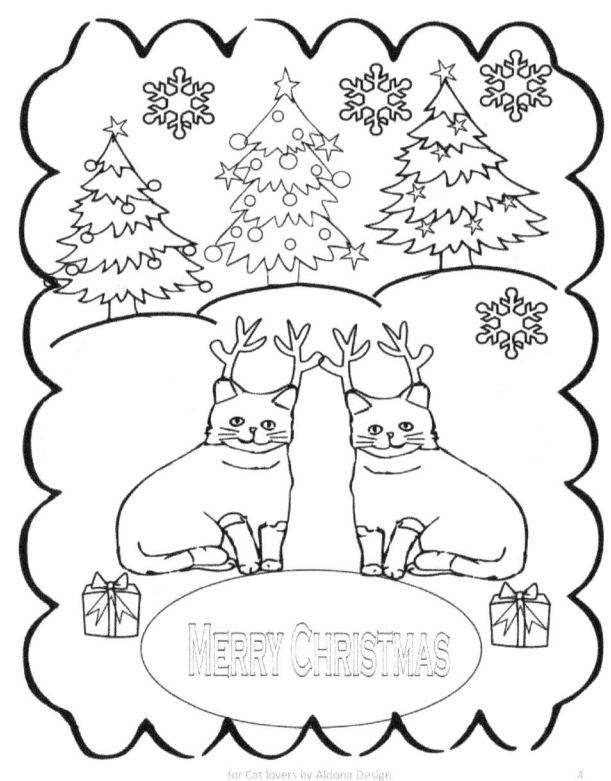

MERRY CHRISTMAS

Reindeer Kitties

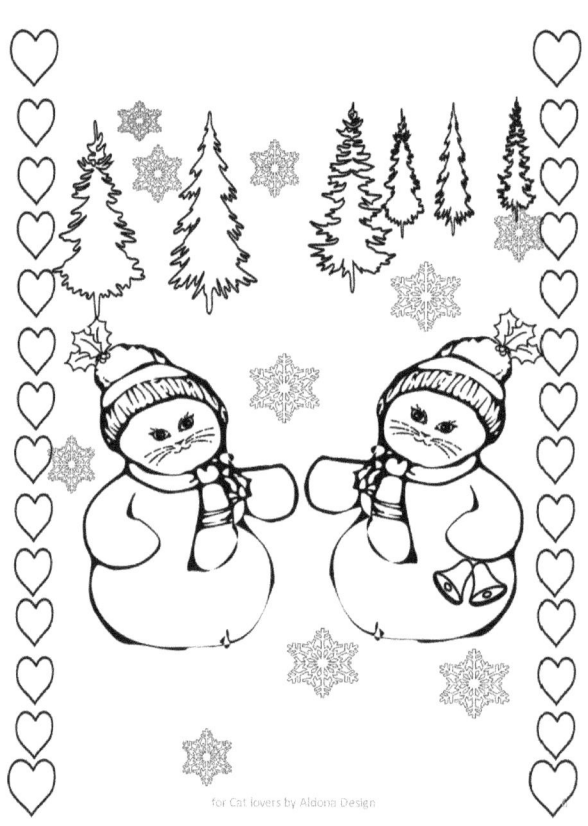

for Cat lovers by Aldona Design

Snowman Kitties

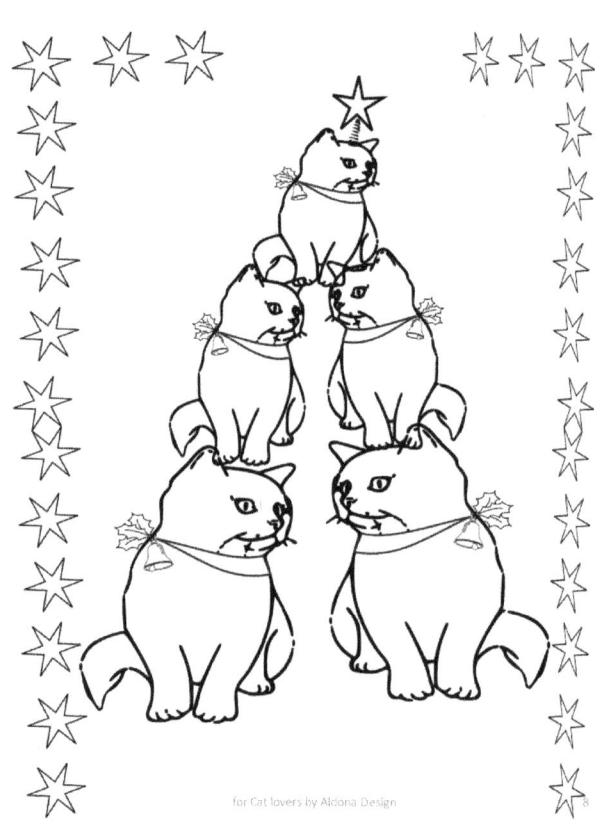

Christmas Tree Kitties

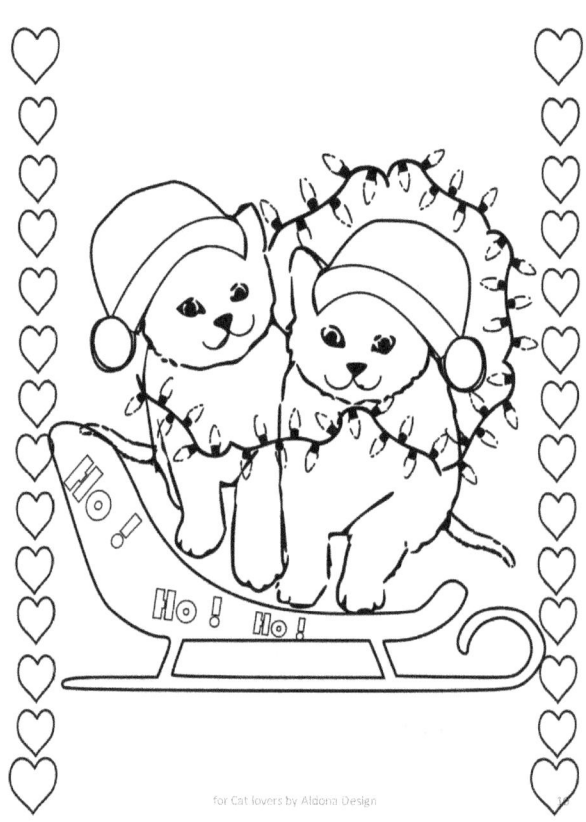

On the Sledge Kitties

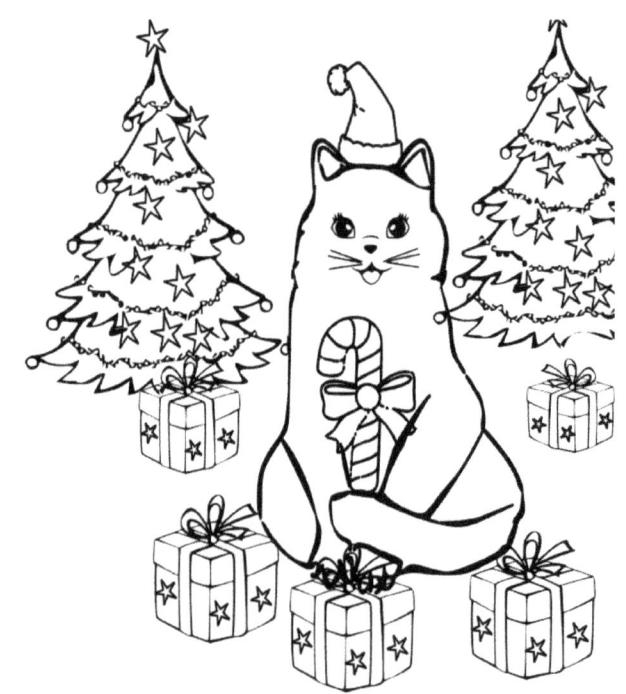

Candy cane Kittie

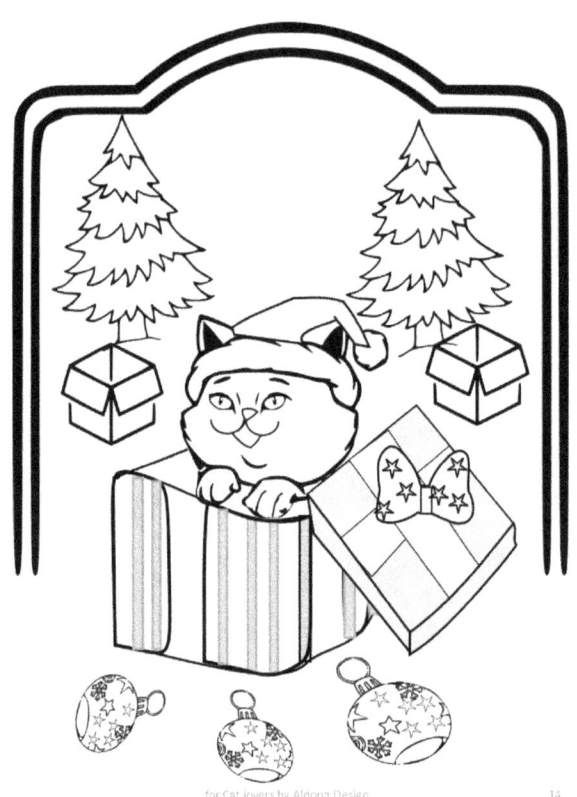

Gift Kittie

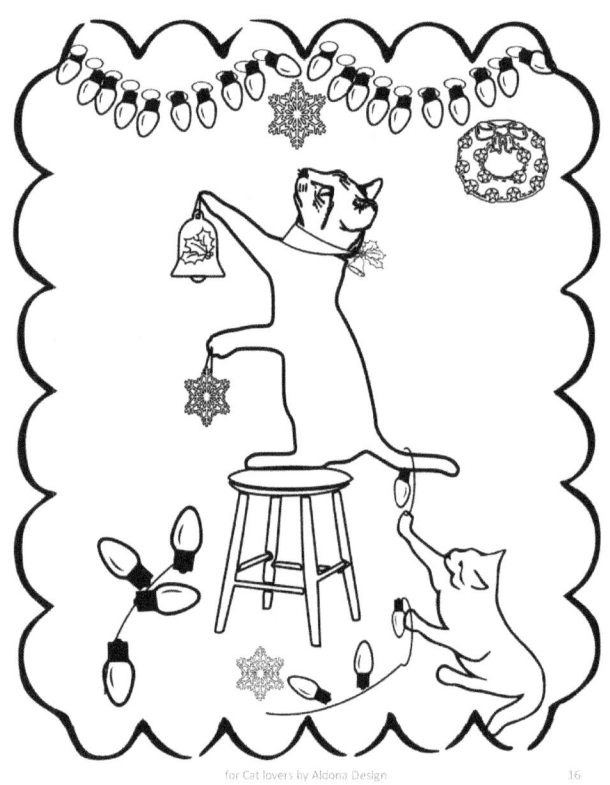

Decorating Kitties

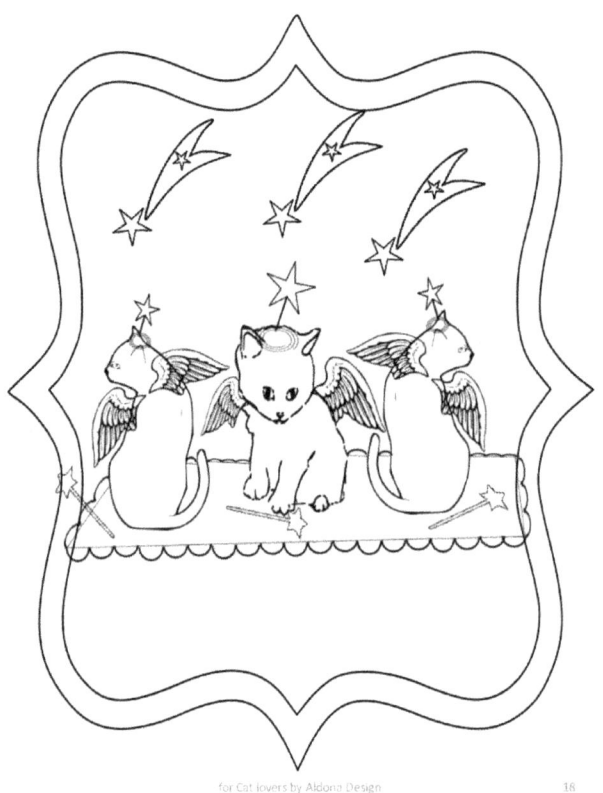

Angel Kitties

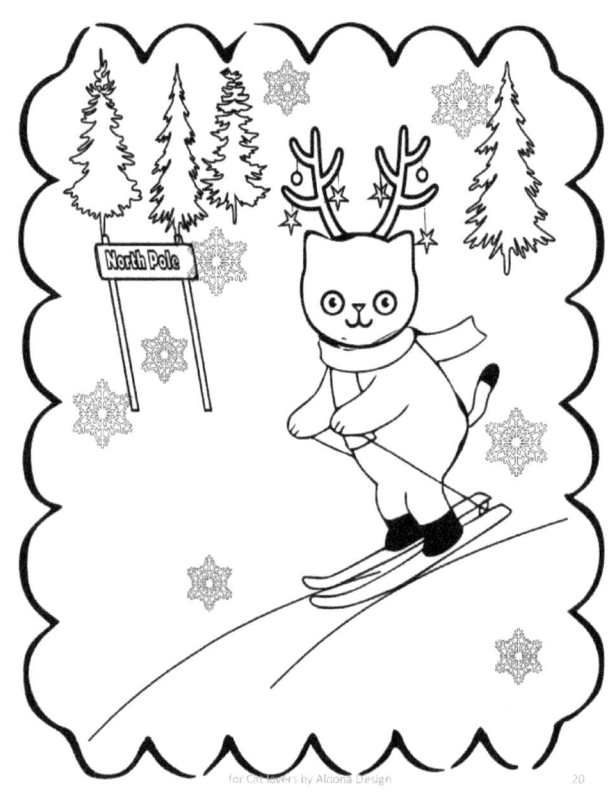

Ski Kittie

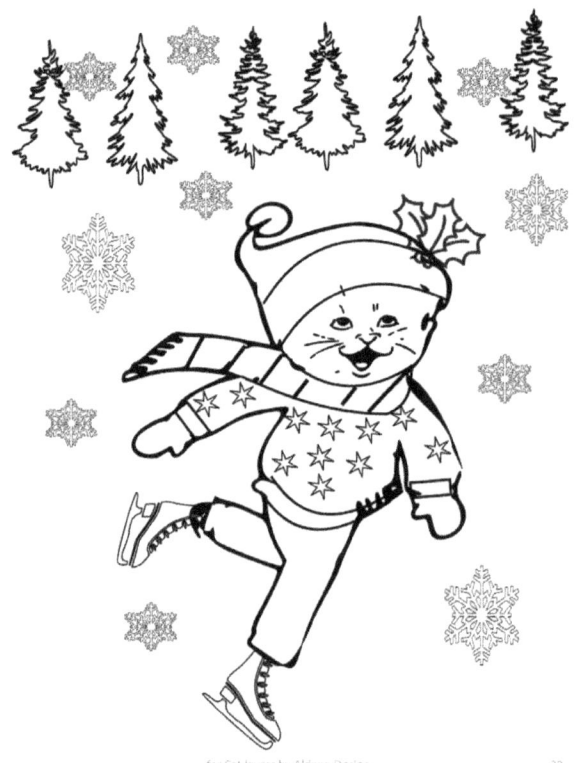

Ice Skating Kittie

for cat lovers by Aldona Design   23

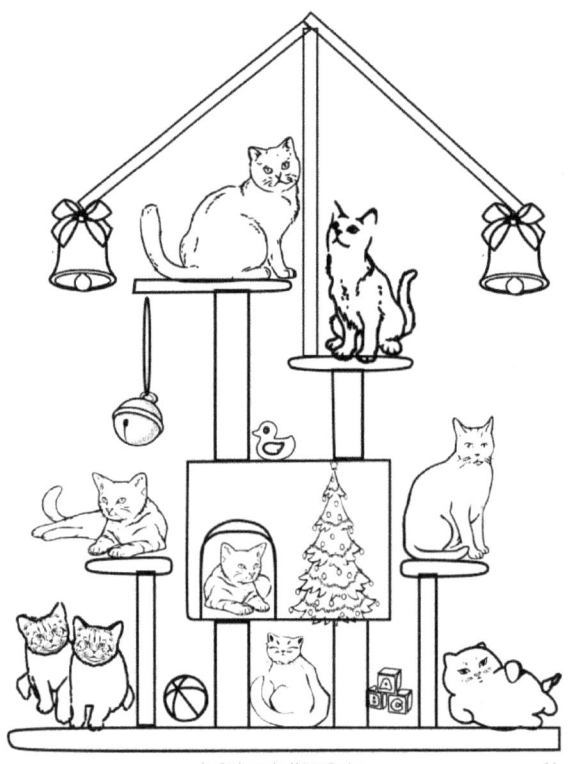

Tree house Kitties

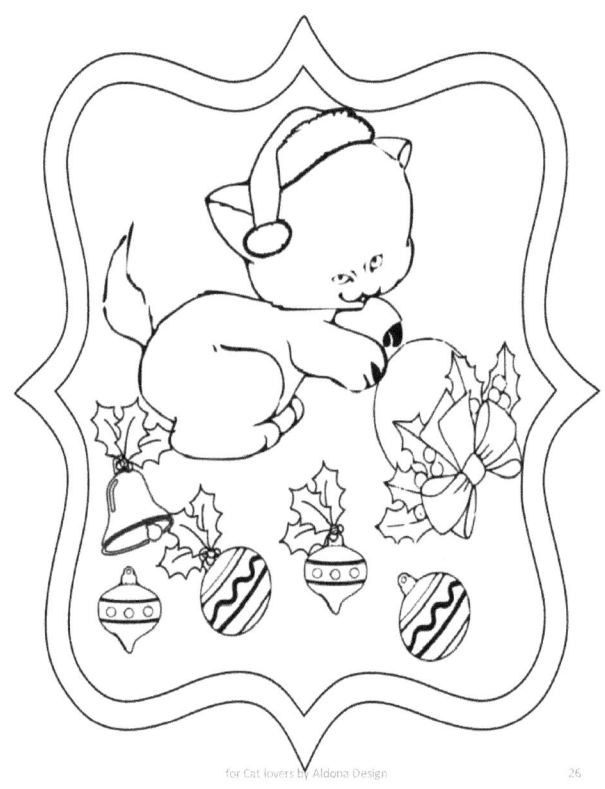

Bauble and Kittie

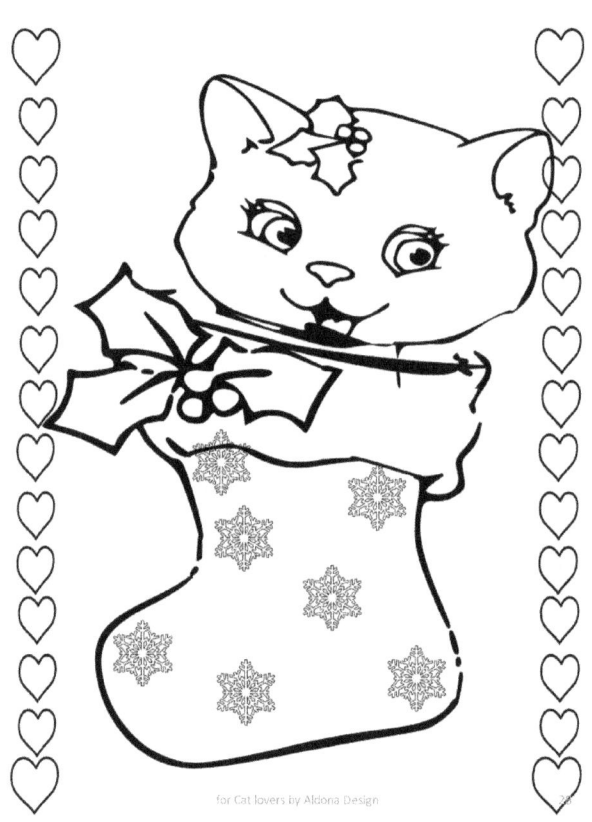

Stocking Kittie

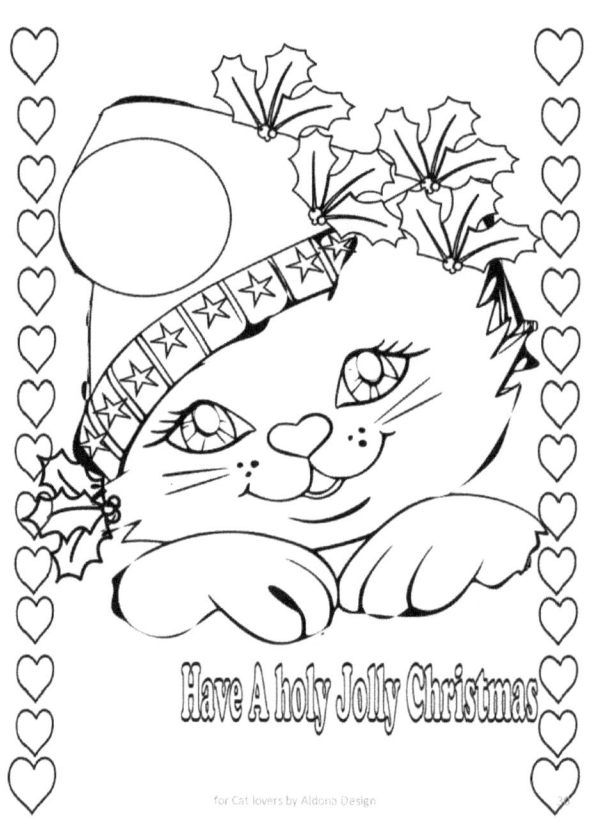

Have A holy Jolly Christmas

Jolly Kittie

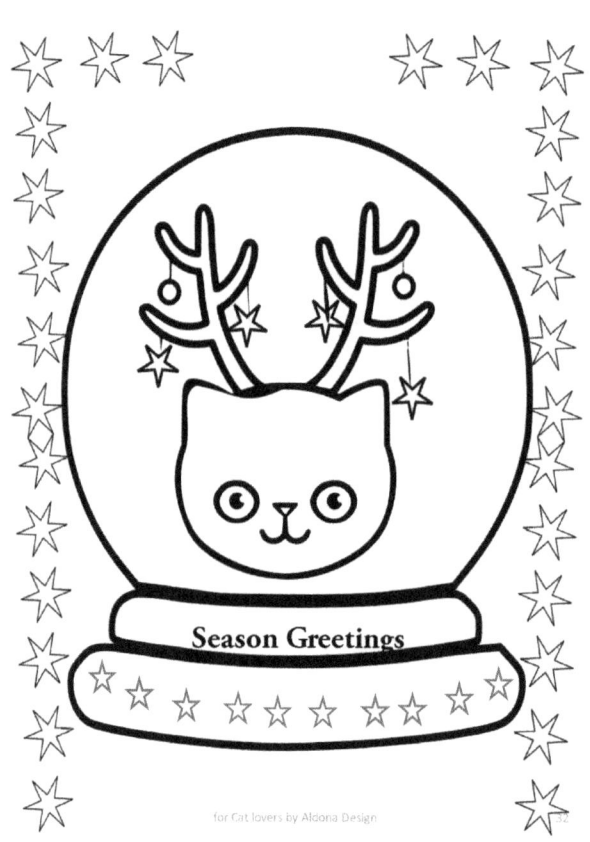

Season Greetings

Snow globe Kittie

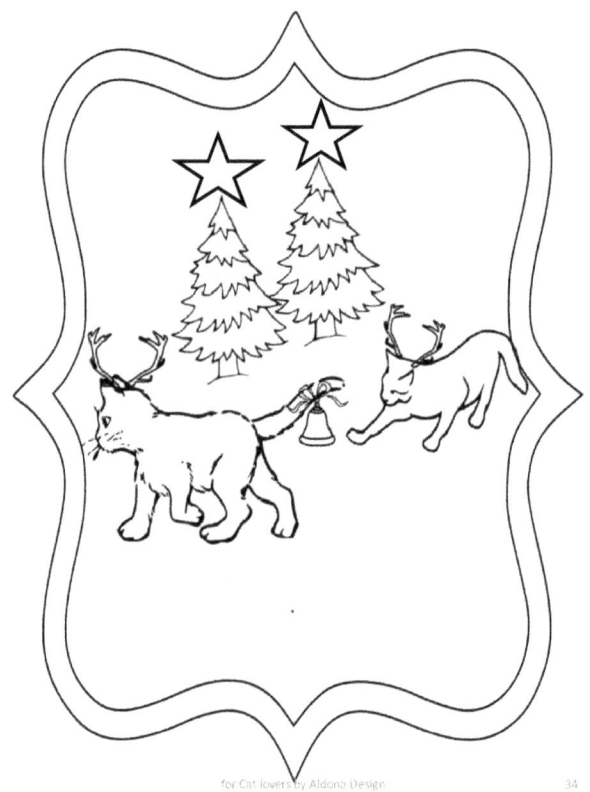

Naughty Kittie

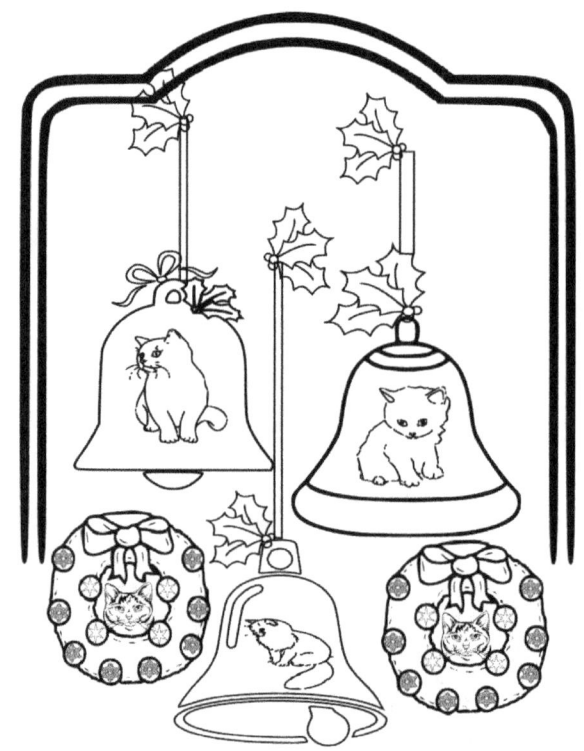

Ornament Kittie

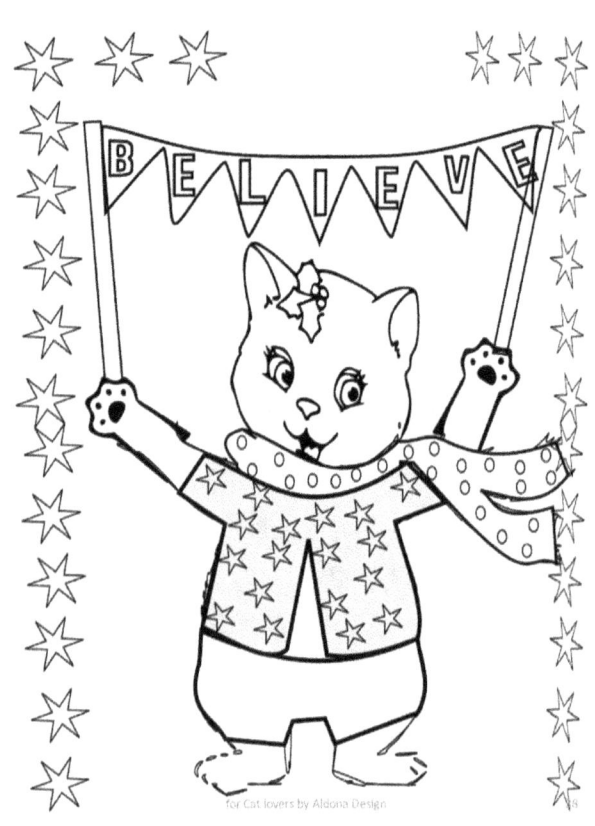

Banner Kittie

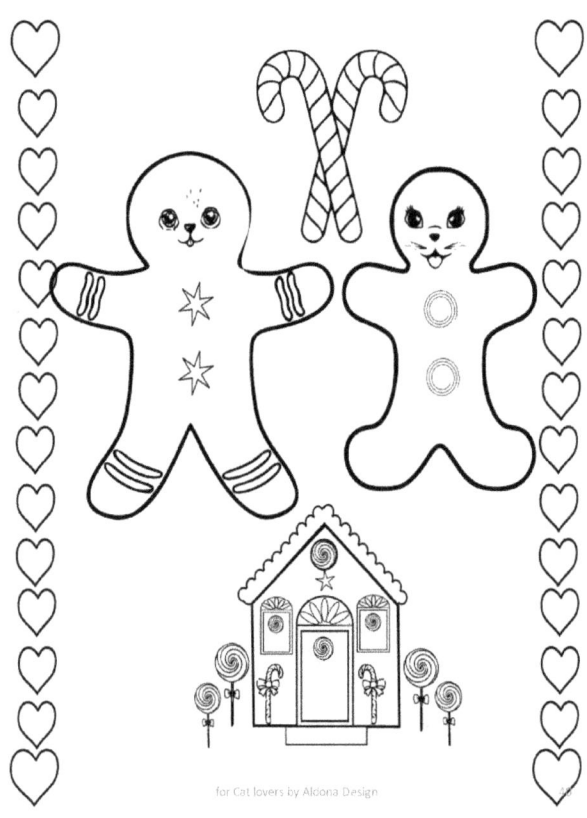

Gingerbread Kittie

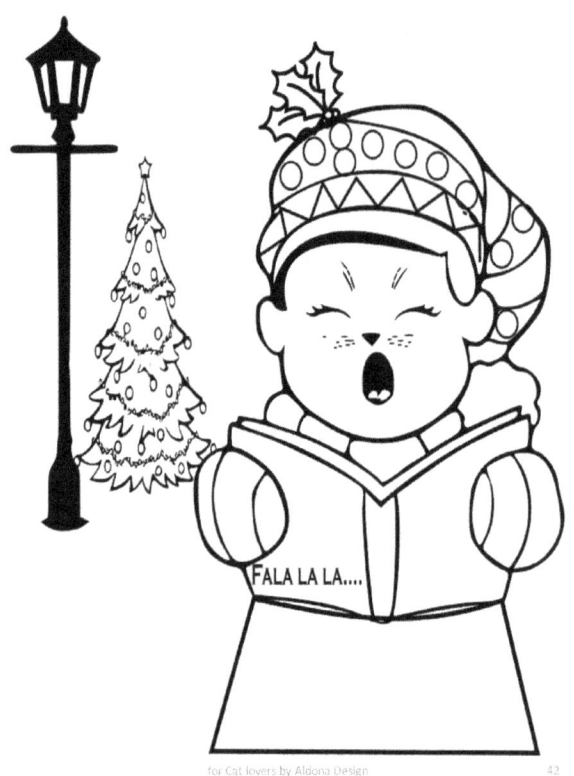

Carol singing Kittie

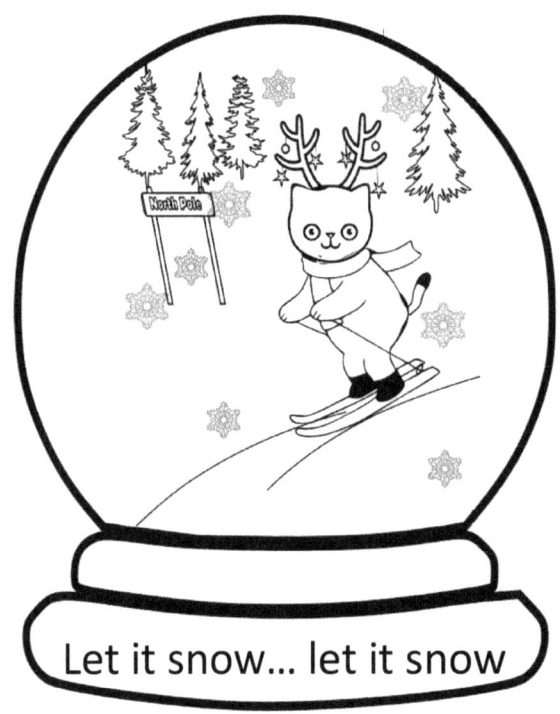

Let it snow... let it snow

Snow globe Kittie

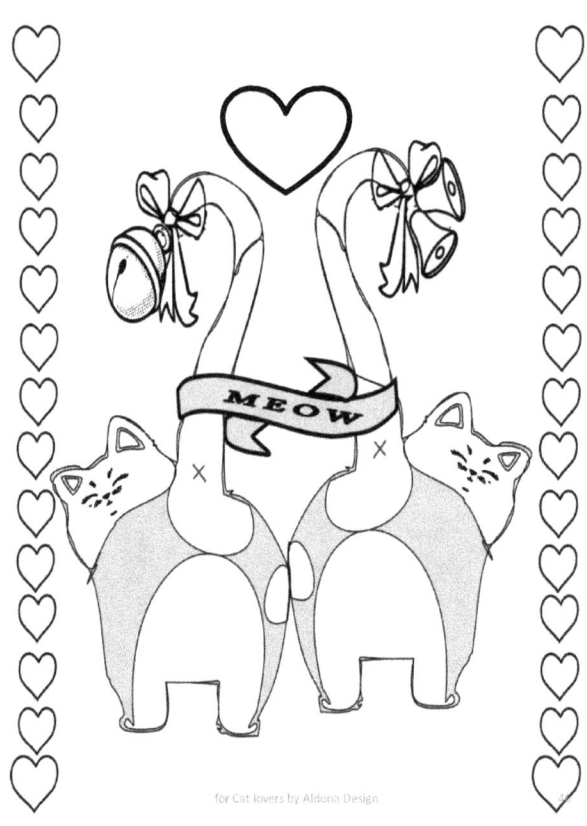

Fancy tail Kitties

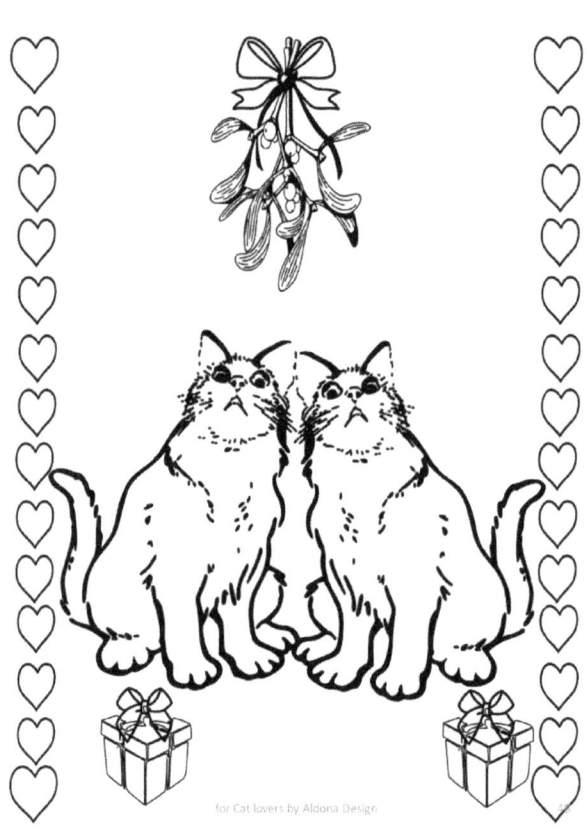

for Cat lovers by Aldona Design

Mistletoe Kitties

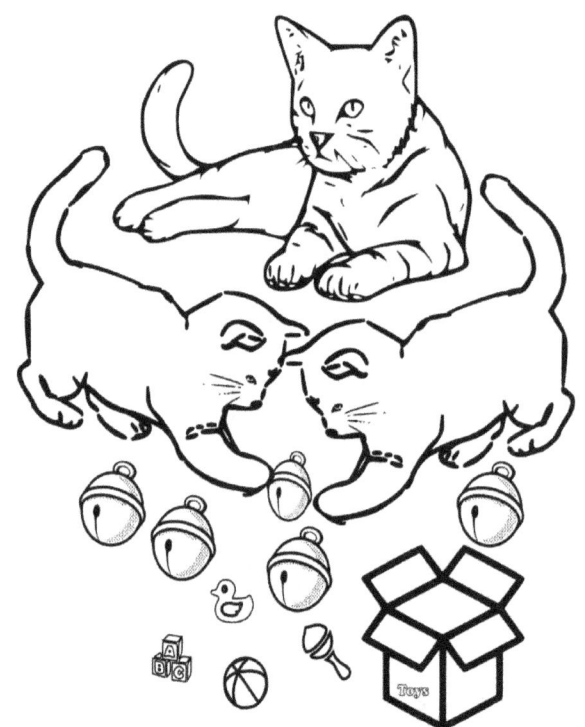

Playful Kitties

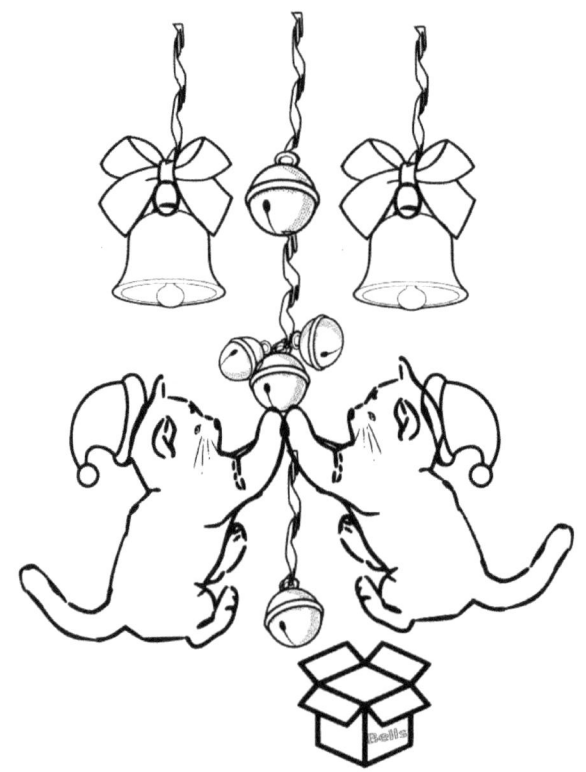

Bell Kitties

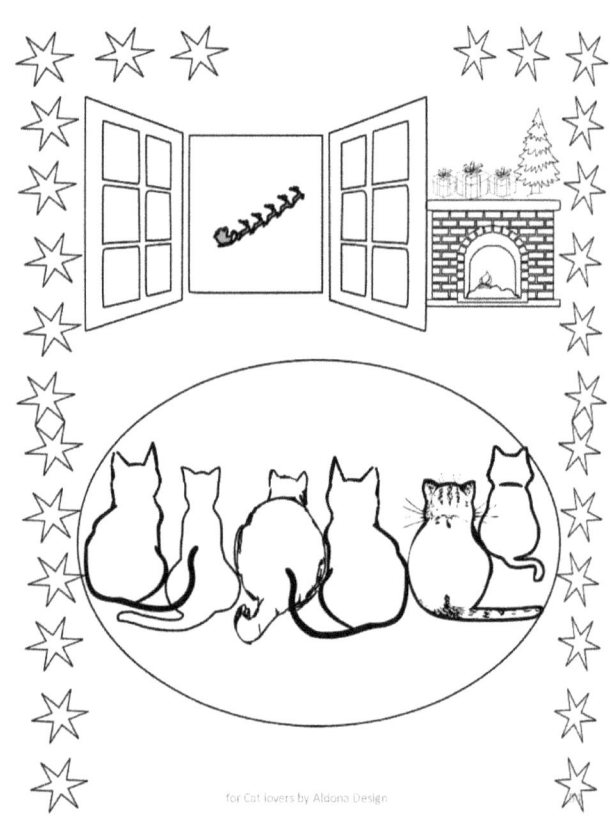

for Cat lovers by Aldona Design

Waiting for Santa Kitties

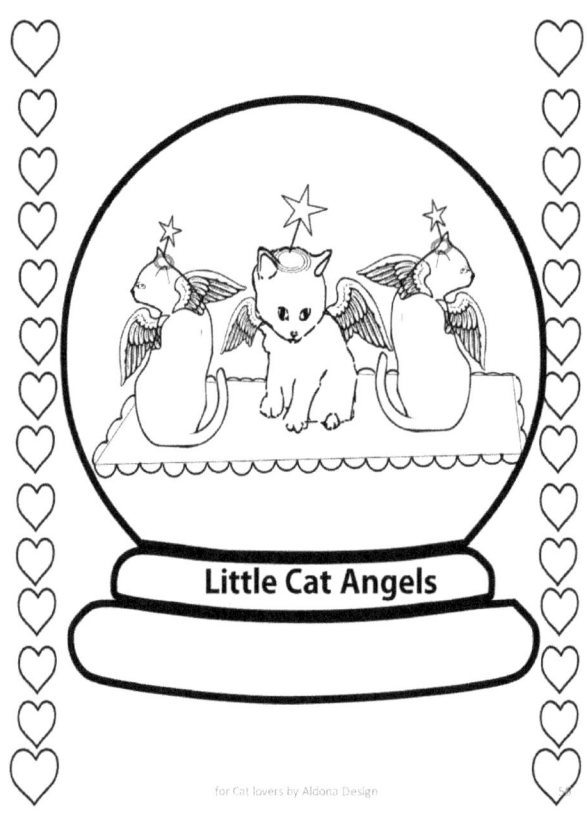

Little Cat Angels

Snow globe Kittie

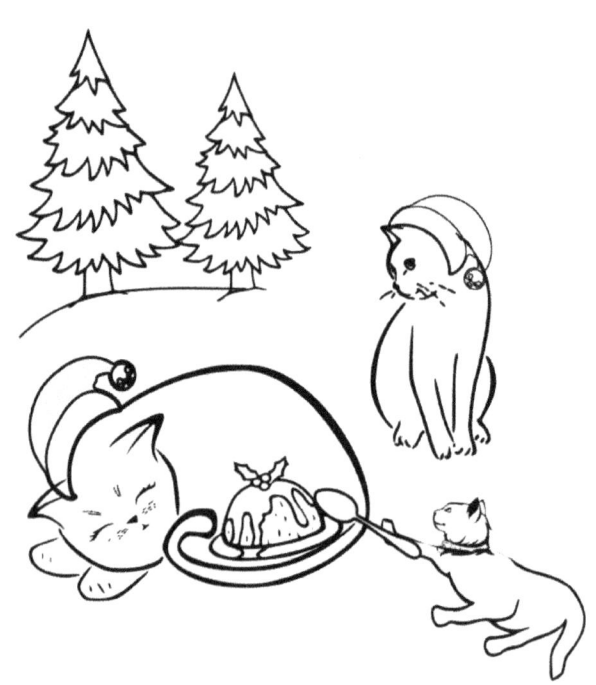

Pudding Kitties

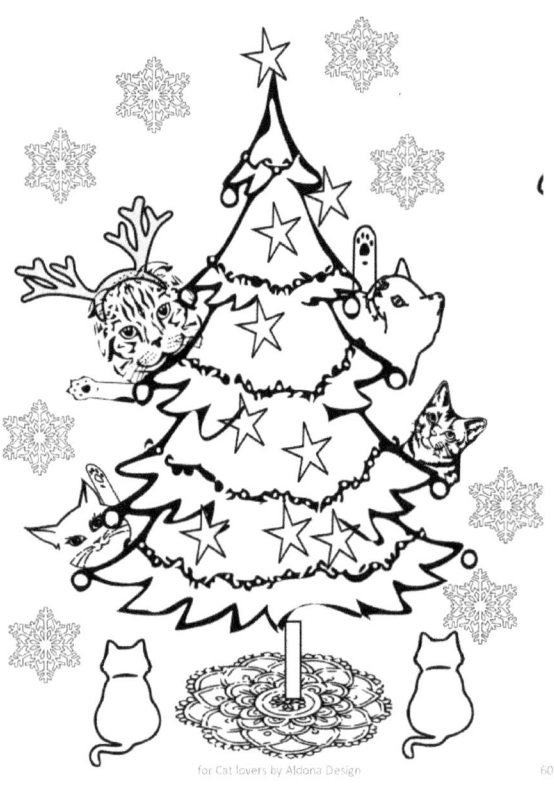

Christmas Tree Kitties

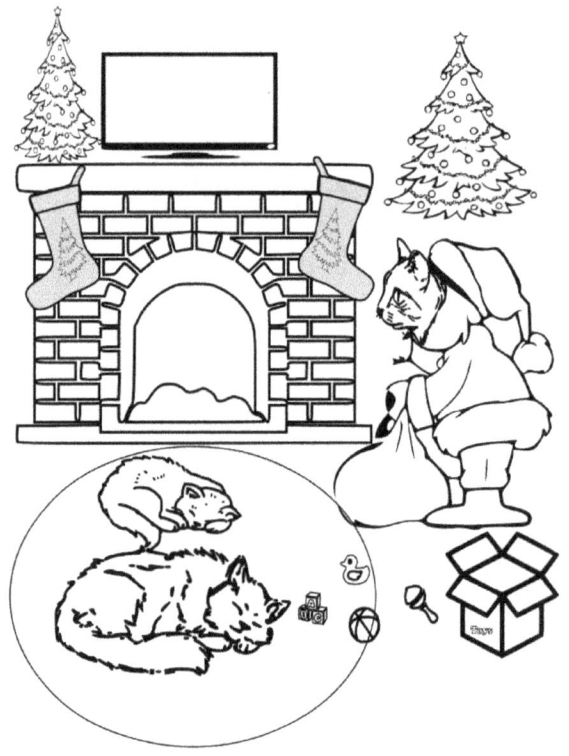

Kitties At Christmas eve

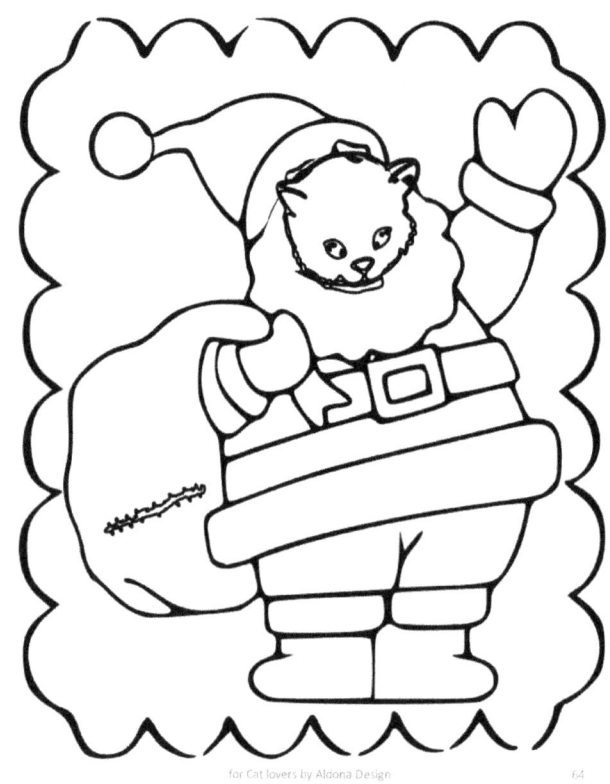

Santa Kittie

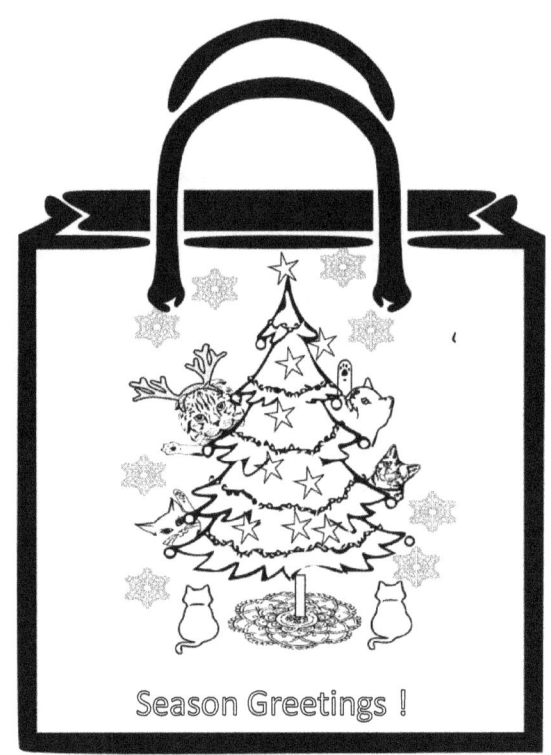

Season Greetings !

Gift bag Kittie

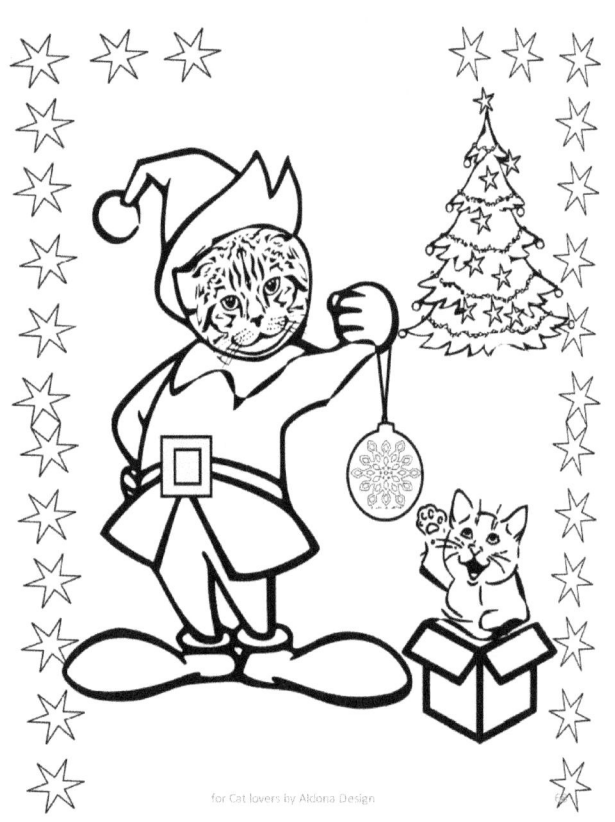

for Cat lovers by Aldona Design

Elf Kittie

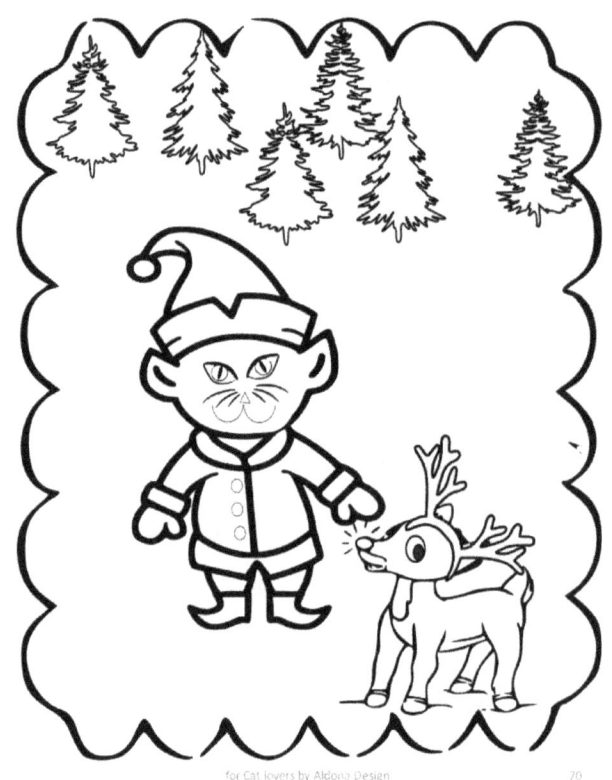

Elf Kittie

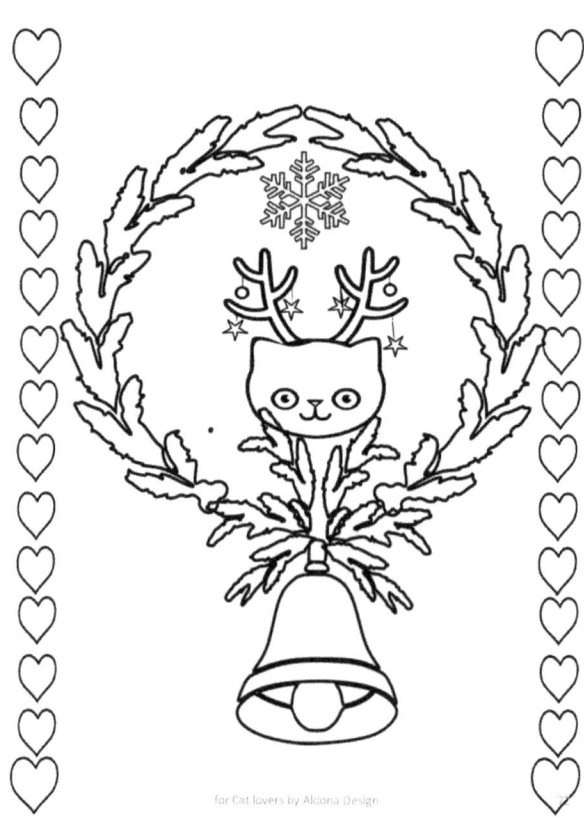

for Cat lovers by Aldona Design

Wreath Kittie

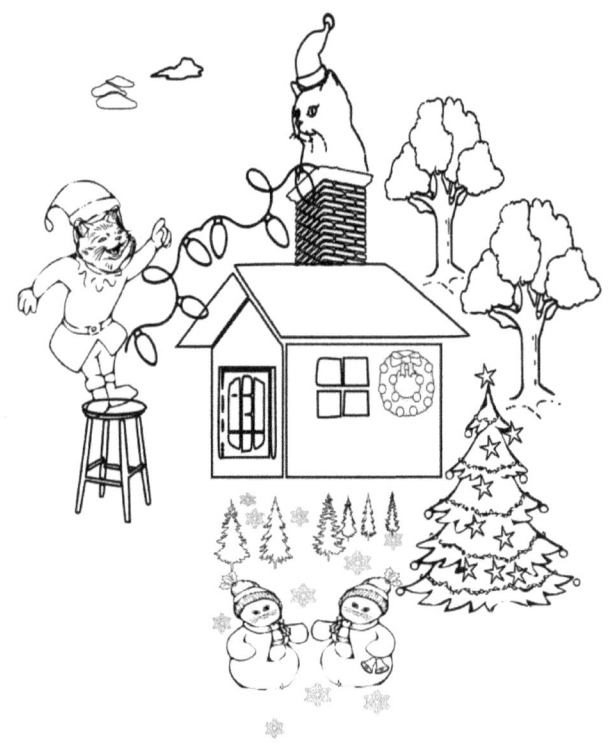

Chimney Kittie

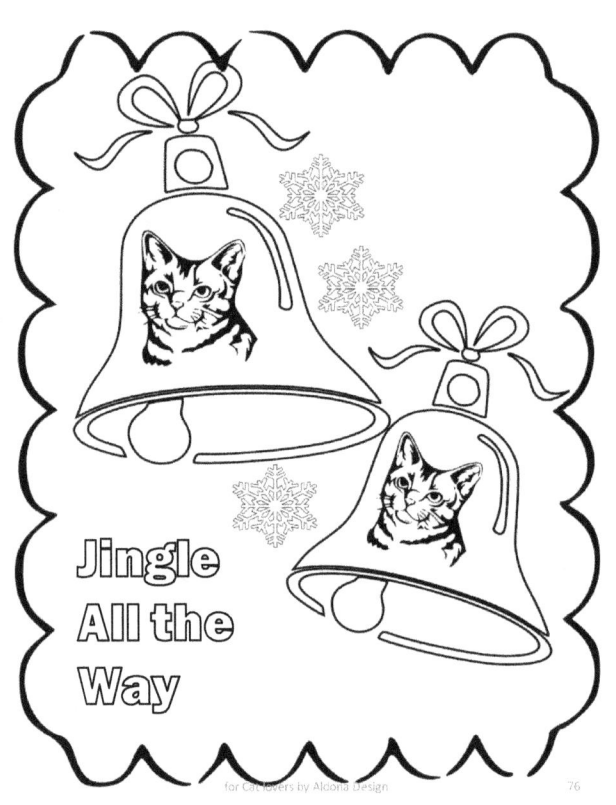

Jingle
All the
Way

Jingle all the way Kitties

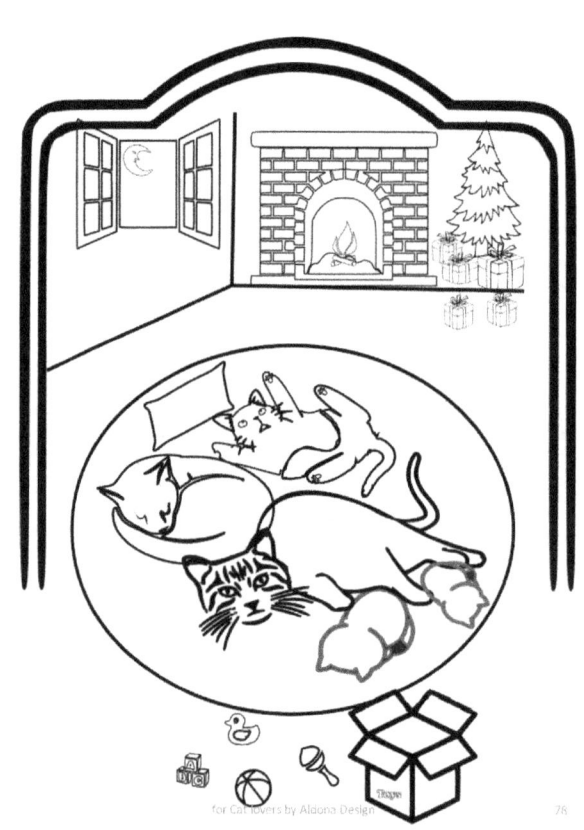

Falling a sleep Kitties

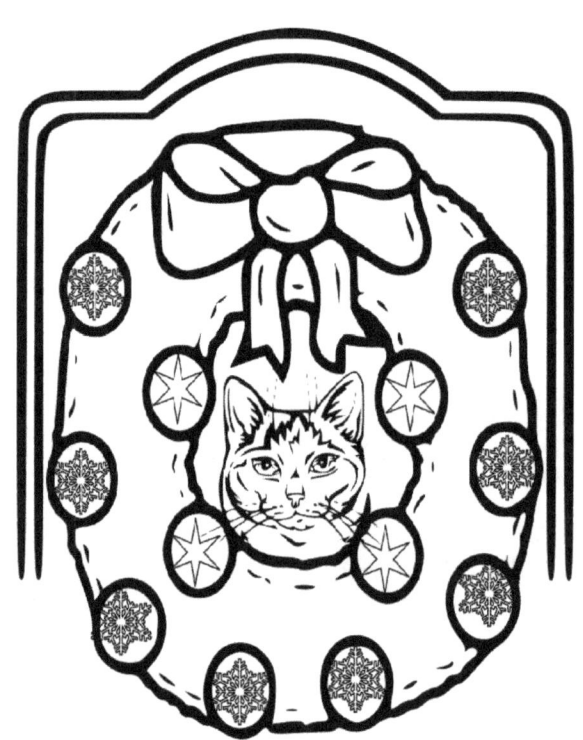

Wreath Kittie

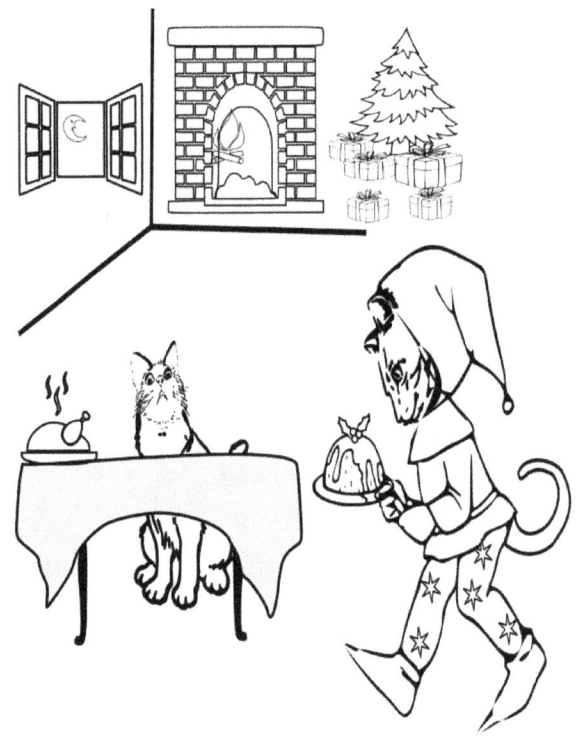

Christmas dinner Kitties

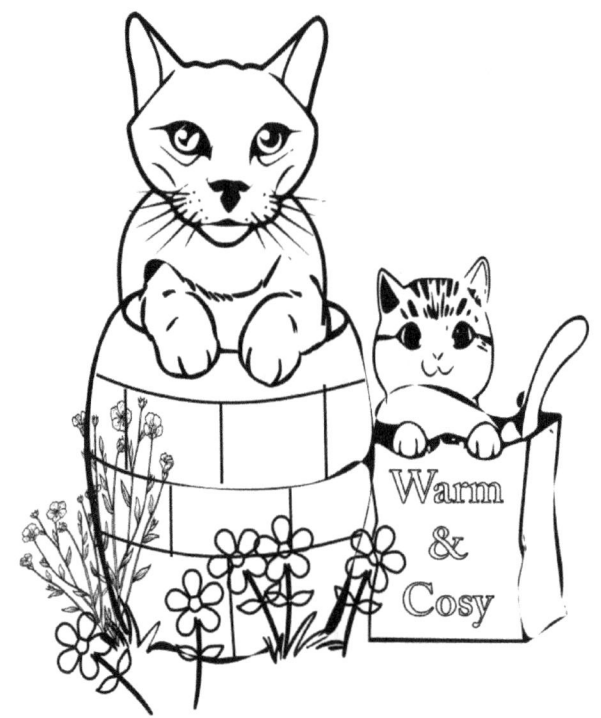

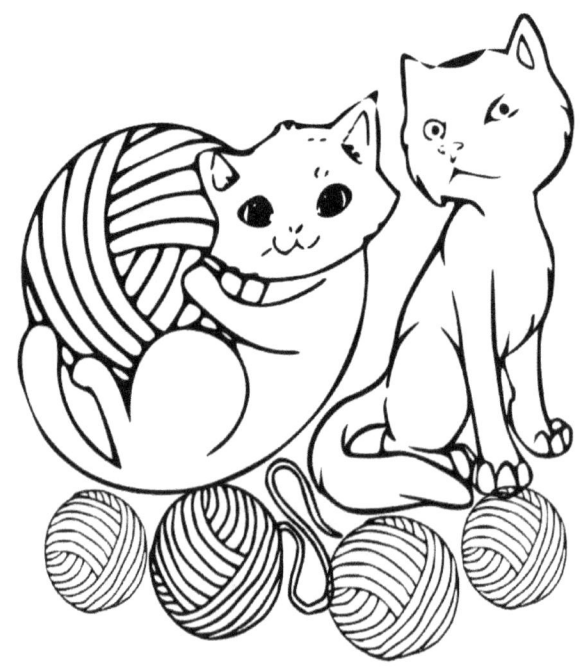

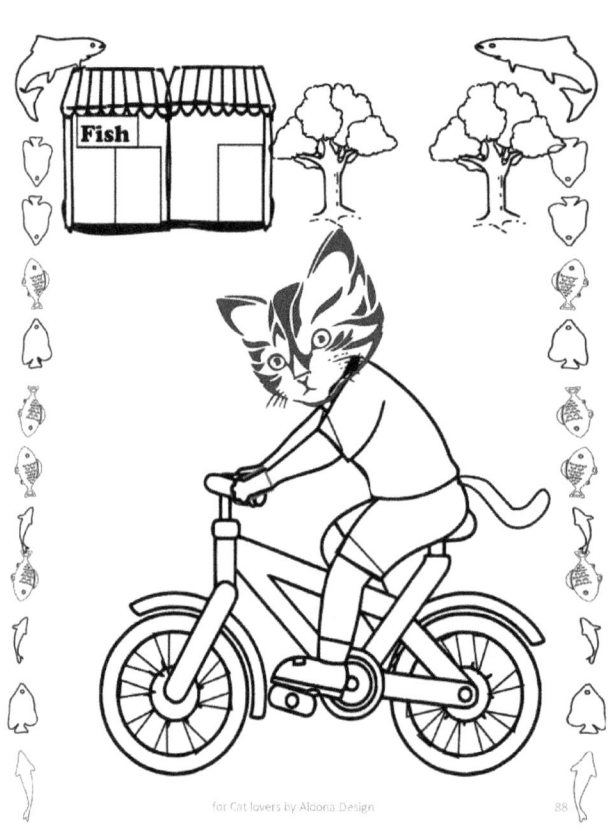

Cycle Kittie

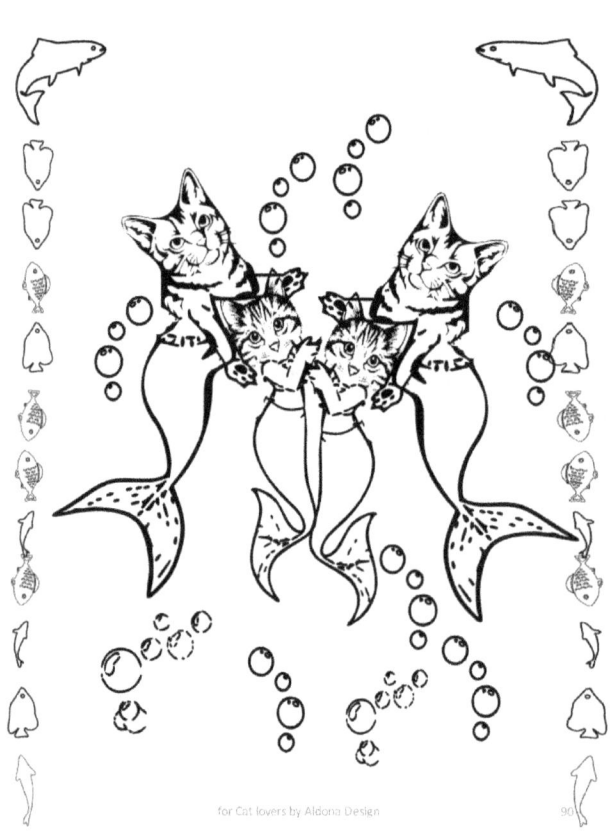

Mermaid Kittie

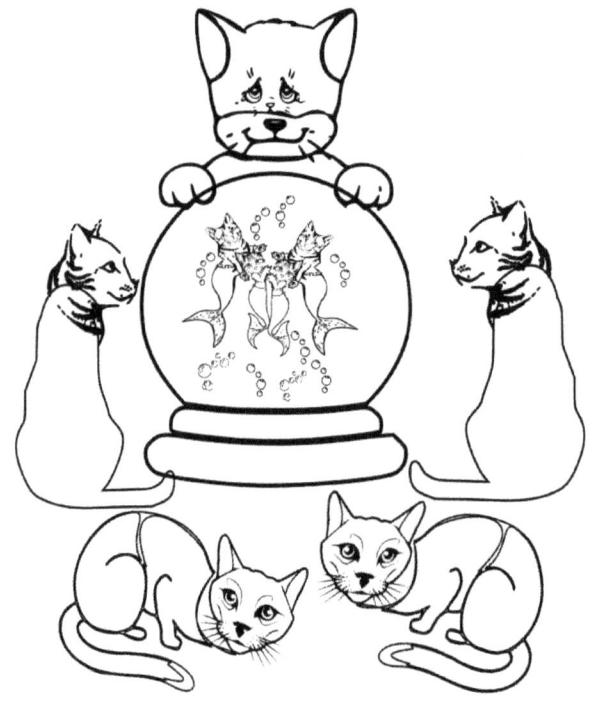

Snow globe Kittie

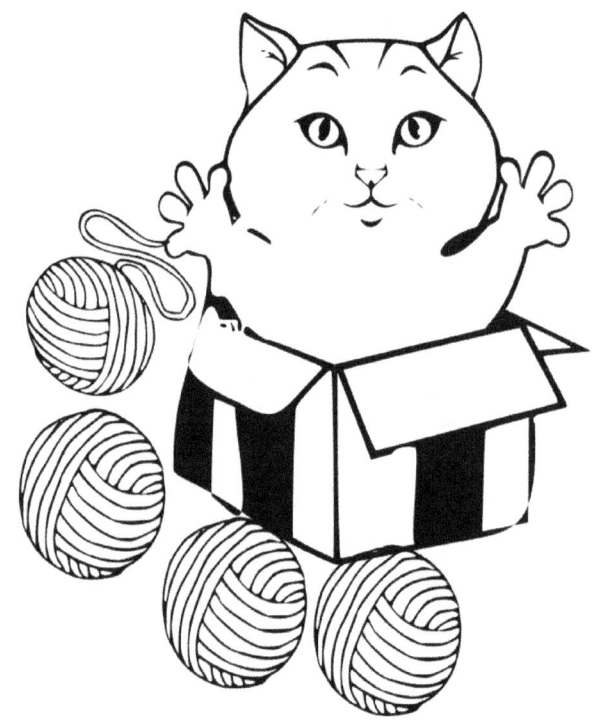

Kittie with ball of yarn

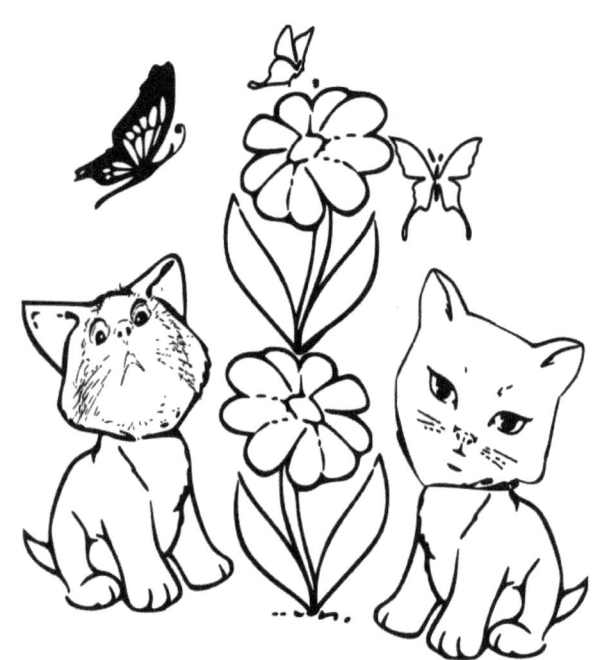

Curious Kittie

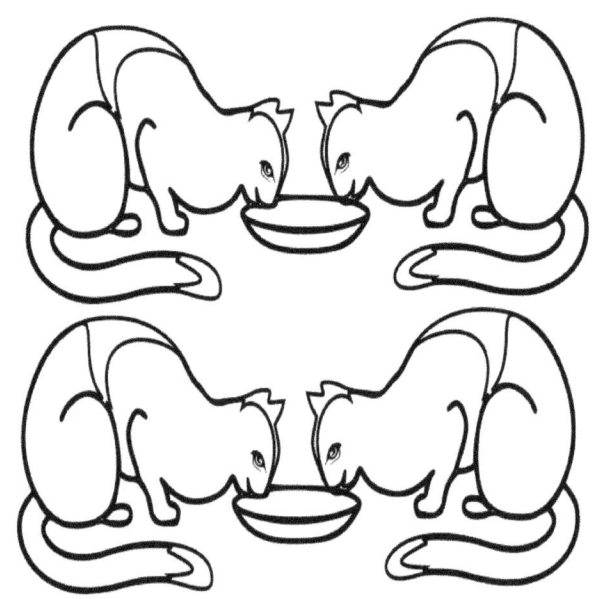

Meal time Kitties

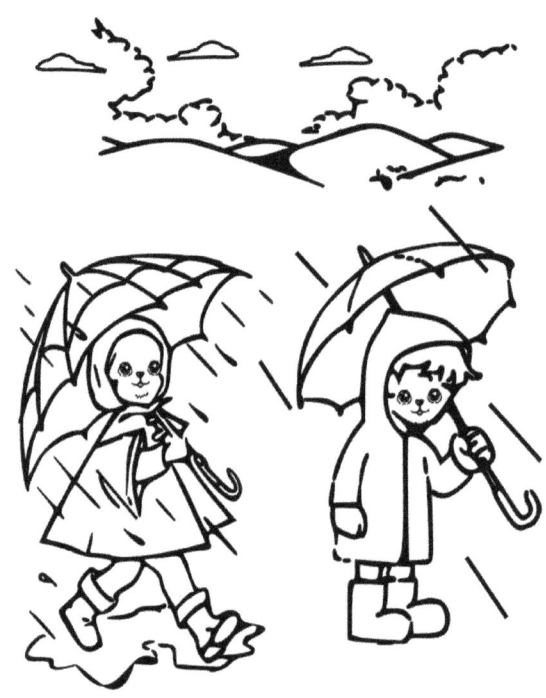

Kitties in the rain

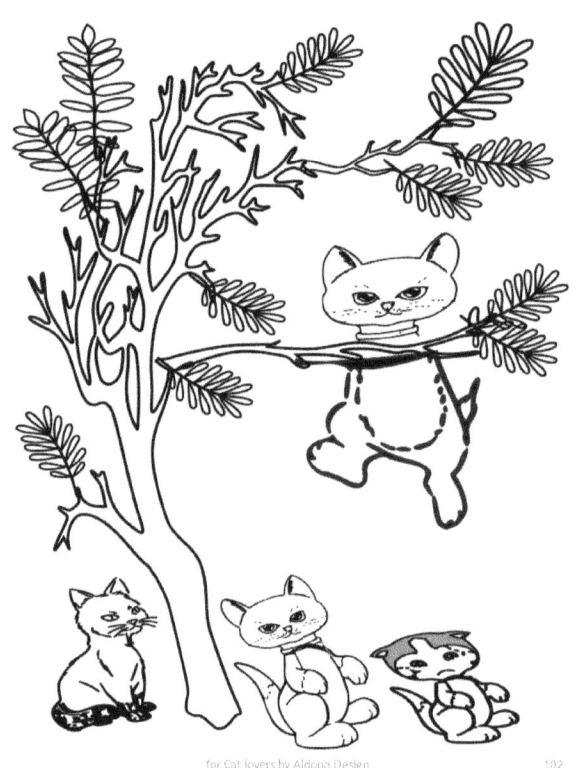

Outdoor Kitties

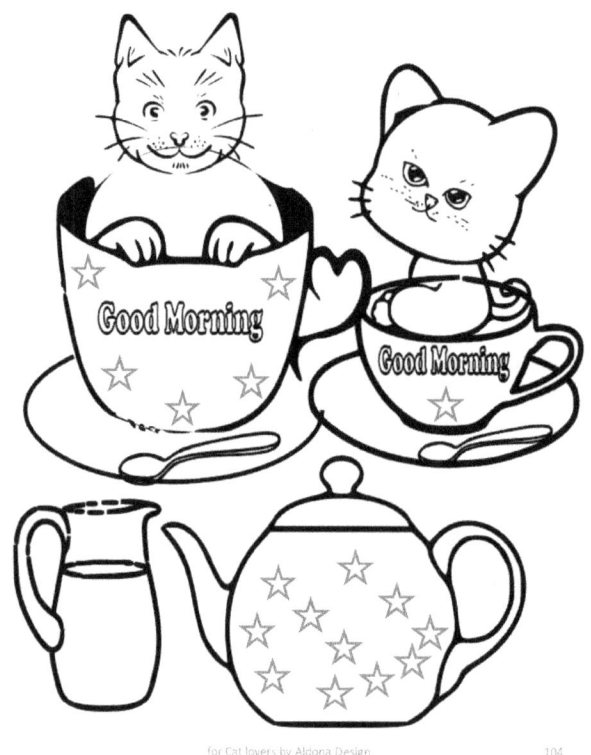

Tea time Kitties

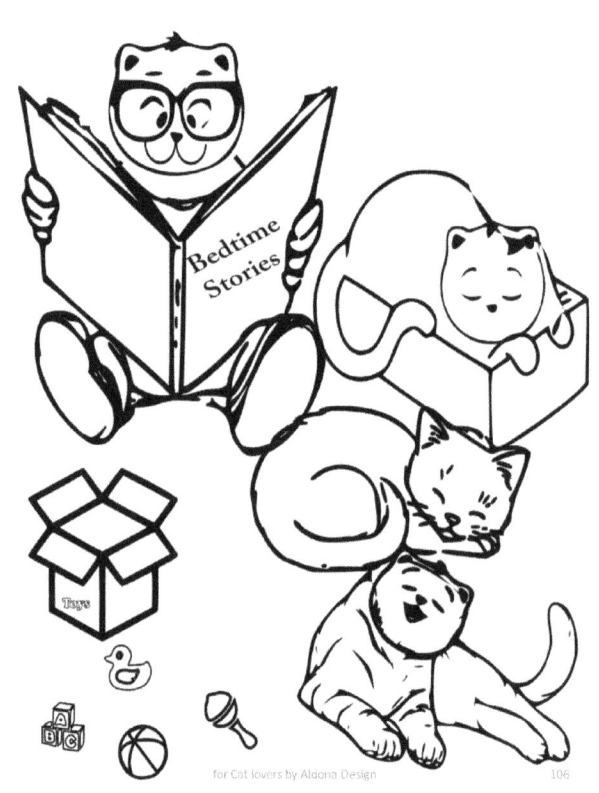

Kitties at bedtime

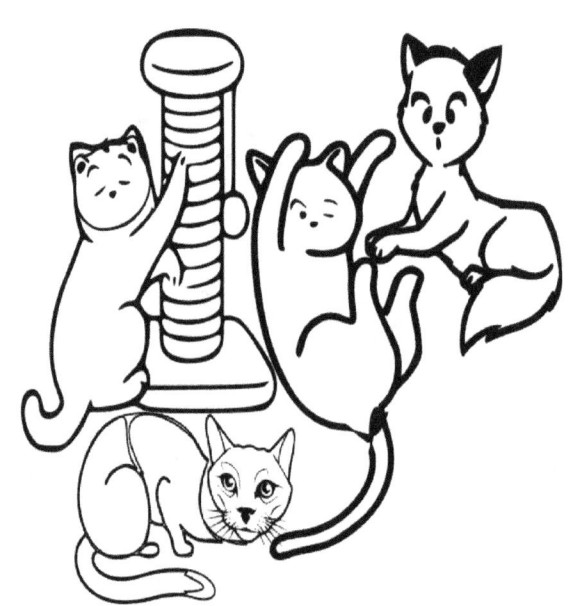

Kitties Scratch & Tickle

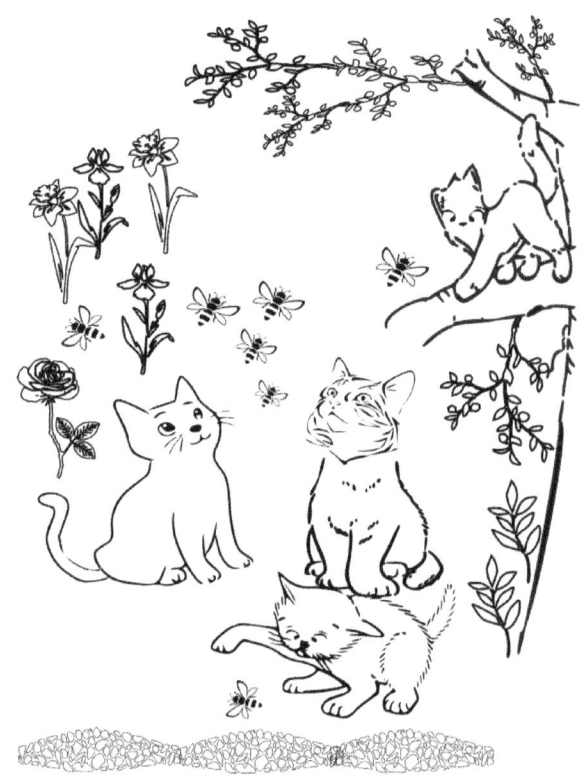

Outdoor Kitties

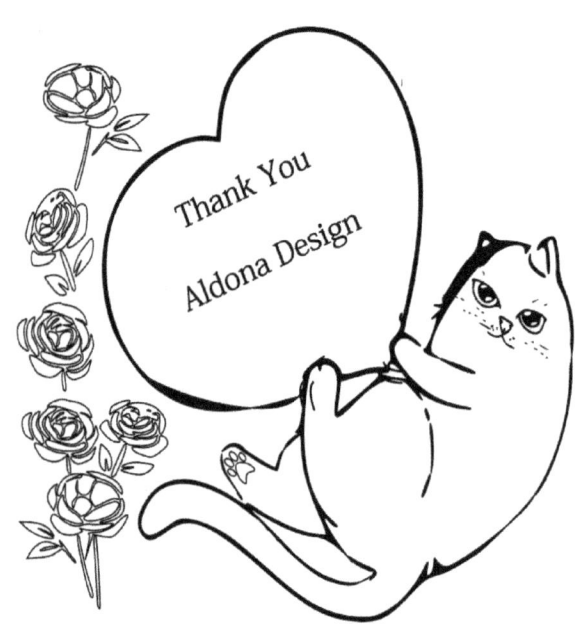

Thank You

Aldona Design

Thankyou Kittie

- List of Colouring books by Aldona Design with their respective ISBN Numbers (Just add the ISBN Number to the link below

- www.amazon.com/gp/product/

- Cute & Adorable Cat Colouring book 9781709770470
- Therapeutic Colouring book (100 pages for Adults) ISBN 1097666700
- Therapeutic Colouring book II (100 pages for Adults)
- ISBN 1080663134
- Therapeutic Colouring book III (100 pages for Adults) ISBN 1687402108
- Therapeutic Coloring book IV: ISBN 1693086476
- Christmas Colouring Books for kids ISBN 1081432489

We would appreciate your Opinion
About this book by leaving a
Review
link follows
Email : **aldonadesign@gmail.com**
Instagram: www.instagram.com/aldona_design
Artwork:- www.redbubble.com/people/aldona

www.amazon.com/author/aldonadesign